RAINTREE BIOGRAPHIES

Eleanor Roosevelt

Amy Stone

RAINTREE STECK-VAUGHN PUBLISHERS
A Harcourt Company
Austin New York
www.raintreesteckvaughn.com

Published by Raintree Steck-Vaughn Publishers, an imprint of Steck-Vaughn Company.

Project Editors: Sean Dolan, Gianna Williams
Production Manager: Richard Johnson
Designed by Ian Winton

Planned and produced by Discovery Books

Library of Congress Cataloging-in-Publication Data
Available upon request.

ISBN 0-7398-5679-0

Printed and bound in China.
1 2 3 4 5 6 7 8 9 0 MID 07 06 05 04 03 02

Acknowledgments
The publishers would like to thank the following for permission to reproduce their pictures:
Cover: Popperfoto; pp.4 & 5 Franklin D. Roosevelt Library; p.6 Corbis; p.7 Franklin D. Roosevelt Library; p.8 Corbis; pp.9 & 10 Franklin D. Roosevelt Library; p.11 Bridgeman Art Library; pp.12 & 13 Popperfoto; pp.14 & 15 Corbis; p.16 Popperfoto; p.17 Corbis; p.18 Popperfoto; pp.19, 20, 21, 22 & 23 Corbis; p.24 Franklin D. Roosevelt Library; p.25 Corbis; pp.26 & 27 Popperfoto; pp.28 & 29 top and bottom Franklin D. Roosevelt Library.

CONTENTS

A Brave and Stubborn Lady

In 1958, the Ku Klux Klan offered a reward to anyone who killed Eleanor Roosevelt, the former first lady of the United States. A secret society of white racists, the Klan hated African Americans. They hated Eleanor Roosevelt because she fought for African Americans' rights. The Klan wanted to stop Eleanor from appearing at a school in Tennessee where she was going to speak about civil rights. Roosevelt, who was 74 years old, had different ideas. Ignoring the threat, she drove at night along dangerous mountain roads through Klan territory to reach the Highlander Folk School.

Books kept Eleanor company during her lonely childhood. In later life, Eleanor often visited the Wiltwyck school in New York, where she read to the students there.

Eleanor (second from right) stands next to her father. He and her mother died while Eleanor and her two younger brothers were still children.

Unlike the Klan, many Americans loved Eleanor Roosevelt. She served as first lady from 1933 to 1945 while married to President Franklin D. Roosevelt. Born in New York on October 11, 1884, into a wealthy family, Anna Eleanor Roosevelt was shy and timid as a youngster. By putting service to others above herself, Roosevelt outgrew her fears. She became known as a great humanitarian, a leader who fought for women, children, the poor, and all minorities.

Facing Your Fears

"You gain strength, courage and confidence by every experience in which you really stop to look fear in the face."

Eleanor Roosevelt,
You Learn By Living

Shy Child, Graceful Woman

Eleanor started life with many advantages. Her family, the Roosevelts, was very wealthy and distinguished. However, before she was 10, both of Eleanor's parents died.

After her parents died, Eleanor's aunt and uncles made sure Eleanor learned how to ride a bike and a horse. Eleanor could make the horse jump over hurdles.

Eleanor moved into her grandmother's New York City home. Grandmother Hall often shut herself in her room, leaving Eleanor all alone. Eleanor's shyness kept her from making many friends, but the many books she read taught her a great deal about the outside world.

Standing Tall

To teach young Eleanor how to stand up straight, Eleanor's grandmother made her walk a mile every day, with her hands held behind her back and a stick across her elbows. Nearly six feet tall as an adult, Roosevelt was known for the grace with which she walked.

When Eleanor was 15, the family sent her to Allenswood, an all-girls' school near London, England. The head of the school, a woman named Marie Souvestre, saw something special in Eleanor. She told her to work hard and praised her when she did. She took Eleanor on trips in Europe, teaching Eleanor how to read train schedules and travel with ease. Slowly, Eleanor began to outgrow her shyness.

Allenswood School, near London, England, in 1900. Eleanor is on the back row, third from the right. Eleanor was popular with her classmates, helping many of them with their homework.

Reaching Out to Others

Eleanor could have spent all her time doing what other rich young women of the day did—attending parties, dances, and teas—when she returned to New York from London in 1902. Instead, she taught dance and exercise classes at a home for young women immigrants in one of the city's poorest neighborhoods. Eleanor even scrubbed the floors at the home, something her wealthy friends would never have done.

In the early 1900s, many children worked long hours in factories such as this textile mill. Eleanor later fought for laws that prevented child labor.

Curious about where many of the residents worked, Eleanor visited nearby factories. The conditions shocked her. Women and children as young as four years old worked six days a week in hot rooms with no fresh air. To protest, Eleanor joined the New York City Consumers' League, a group that called public attention to conditions in the factories.

By 1905, Eleanor had fallen in love with Franklin D. Roosevelt, a distant cousin who hoped to one day become president of the United States. Eleanor showed Franklin the slums of New York, opening his eyes to a hidden world and his heart to people who struggled just to survive.

Eleanor Roosevelt in her wedding dress, March 17, 1905.

ELEANOR'S WEDDING

When Eleanor married Franklin D. Roosevelt on March 17, 1905, her uncle, Theodore Roosevelt, who was then president of the United States, gave her away. After President Roosevelt left the wedding party, so did most of the guests. They had come to see the president, not Eleanor and Franklin!

DUTY COMES FIRST

Eleanor and Franklin had six children between the years 1906 and 1916. Their third child, Franklin, Jr., died of influenza when he was still a baby. During this time, Eleanor devoted herself to taking care of her children.

Eleanor holds baby James while her husband, Franklin, holds their daughter Anna. Although Eleanor adored her young children, she longed for a career outside the home.

On April 6, 1917, not long after Eleanor gave birth to her last child, the United States entered World War I. From 1914 to 1918 many countries around the world fought in this war, at a cost of millions of lives.

This World War I poster encourages Americans to help the war effort by volunteering for the Red Cross. Eleanor responded to this call.

In the United States, many young men joined the armed forces, while other Americans looked for different ways to help their country. With five youngsters to care for, Eleanor still found time to work at a Red Cross stand that provided coffee and snacks for traveling U.S. soldiers.

A year after World War I ended, Eleanor's Grandmother Hall died. A year later, in 1920, the Nineteenth Amendment to the U.S. Constitution gave women the right to vote. Eleanor decided to join the newly formed League of Women Voters. The League helped women register to vote and educated them about politics and the people running for office.

Too Busy Helping Others

Early one morning in 1918, while working at a Red Cross stand, Eleanor cut her finger down to the bone. Instead of going to the hospital, she stayed at the stand all day, wrapping her bleeding finger in one handkerchief after another.

Conquering Fears

In 1921 Franklin Roosevelt contracted polio. Polio is an infectious disease, caused by a virus. It left Roosevelt almost totally paralyzed for a time. He would never regain the use of his legs.

At the time, the illness seemed as if it would destroy Franklin's political career. Although only 38, he had already been a member of the New York state senate, assistant secretary of the Navy, and the Democratic nominee for vice-president in 1920.

A talented writer, organizer, and leader, Eleanor (third from right) loved working with other women in the Democratic National Party.

A rich and powerful woman, Sara D. Roosevelt shared her home and strong opinions with Franklin and Eleanor.

Fanklin's mother, Sara, begged him to give up his political career. Eleanor, meanwhile, encouraged him to continue in politics. While Franklin received treatment in Warm Springs, Georgia, Eleanor made public appearances on his behalf all over New York state. At first, her voice and hands shook when she made speeches, but she soon learned to be a very effective public speaker.

Fighting over Franklin

The arguments between Sara and Eleanor about Franklin's future could be intense. Once Eleanor got so mad that she slammed the door that connected her home to Sara's. Then, by herself, she hauled a huge cabinet across the room to bar the door.

A Teacher and Friend

In the 1920s, Eleanor supported new laws that shortened women's work weeks, raised wages, and ended child labor. This work also allowed Eleanor to meet many interesting women. One of these was Marian Dickerman, a teacher and vice principal at Todhunter School, a private girls' school in New York City. Dickerman invited Eleanor to work there, too. From 1926 until 1933, Eleanor taught English, history, and government at Todhunter School. She did it so well that many students considered her their best teacher.

Always interested in the well-being of children, Eleanor visits the Progressive School of the Vassar Institute of Euthenics in Poughkeepsie, New York.

Succeeding on behalf of all women

"I knew that as the only woman, I'd better be better than anybody else... I knew that if I...failed, it would not be just my failure; it would be the failure of all women...."

Eleanor Roosevelt, as quoted in the PBS television documentary ***The American Experience: Eleanor Roosevelt***

In 1925, Franklin had a small stone house built for Eleanor near the Hudson River in Hyde Park, New York, not far from their home. Val-Kill, as it became known, gave Eleanor a sanctuary where she and her friends could discuss events and ideas. Eleanor said Val-Kill reminded her of Allenswood School. Today Val-Kill is the only U.S. National Historic site to honor a first lady.

Eleanor and some women friends turned part of her Val-Kill home into a furniture factory. Eleanor (left) proudly displays one of the well-made chairs.

The Eleanor and Franklin Team

Franklin Roosevelt was elected governor of New York in 1928. Because Franklin's disability made it difficult for him to make public appearances, Eleanor often made them for him. She visited state schools, prisons, and hospitals. When Franklin asked if one of the places she visited was serving the right foods, Eleanor said, "Oh, yes, I looked at the menus." "I didn't ask you about the menus," Franklin replied. "I asked you what the food was like. You should have looked in the pots on the stove." "After that," Eleanor said, "I was very much better as an observer."

Eleanor's travels throughout New York during her husband's terms as governor put her in touch with New Yorkers. Her caring manner impressed them, and many wrote her for help.

The duties of a political wife required Eleanor to attend many formal events, but she preferred putting her energy into social causes.

When her husband ran for governor of New York in 1928, Eleanor wrote many of his speeches.

TRYING TO HELP

One woman asked Eleanor to free her son from jail. "When she found out I could not...," Eleanor remembered, "she begged that I go see him, which I did. Now she begs that I go weekly...!"

While the wife of the governor, Eleanor continued to teach at the Todhunter School. She could have asked for a fancy state car to drive her from the governor's residence in the state capital of Albany, New York, to the school in New York City. Instead, Eleanor took the train. She never thought of herself as a special person.

First Lady? No Thanks!

On October 24, 1929, the New York stock market crashed. The Great Depression that followed lasted for 10 years and crippled the U.S. economy. Nine thousand banks closed, wiping out the savings accounts of nine million people almost overnight. Factories and businesses shut down as well, putting 15 million Americans out of work. Between 1934 and 1937 severe drought destroyed the livelihoods of many farmers in an area of the Midwest that became known as the Dust Bowl.

Many Americans lost their jobs and homes during the Great Depression of 1929–1939. Soup kitchens like this one helped many hungry people survive.

Eleanor joins coal miners on a ride deep into a coal mine. Eleanor's efforts improved Americans' working conditions and raised their wages.

In 1932 Franklin Roosevelt ran for president of the United States, promising to lead the country out of the Depression. The federal government should create jobs and provide food and shelter for all Americans, he proclaimed. Eleanor agreed. She did not want to be just the first lady, or wife of the U.S. president. First ladies ran the social calendar of the White House. Eleanor knew such a job would bore her.

Fearing the Future

When Franklin Roosevelt ran for president in 1932, Eleanor had a career of her own. She feared, however, that the country would not accept a working woman as first lady. "As I saw it," she said, "[a victory] meant the end of any personal life of my own."

The Autobiography of Eleanor Roosevelt

A New Kind of First Lady

In 1932, Franklin D. Roosevelt was elected president. Two days after he took office, first lady Eleanor Roosevelt amazed the nation. On March 6, 1933, she invited 35 women reporters to the White House. First ladies were not supposed to talk with reporters. People thought women were too "gentle" and "nervous" to handle the pressure of reporters' questions. But Eleanor was not a shy girl.

Franklin D. Roosevelt is inaugurated as president of the United States on March 4, 1933.

Eleanor quickly proved that she could handle questions, and that she had interesting things to say. Eleanor told reporters her husband's back-to-work programs should include women, young people, and African Americans—not just white men.

Eleanor takes the podium on Women's Day at the 1933 Chicago World Fair. By then, Eleanor had become a confident and popular speaker.

As first lady, Eleanor kept in touch with poor and ordinary people all across the nation. She talked with coal miners and sharecroppers. Everywhere, she approached out-of-work people, wanting to hear how they were getting by. Eleanor's listening ear was as important as Franklin's programs in creating the feeling among Americans that the government cared about them and their problems.

Children's Letters

Many children barely survived the Depression. One in five did not have enough to eat, and many lacked warm clothes for the winter. One 13-year-old girl wrote Eleanor, "I have to stay out of school because I have no books or clothes to ware [wear]." Eleanor received so many letters from young people she could not write personal replies. Instead, she helped start government programs to assist them.

A Friend to the Poor

Seeing their educated parents and relatives lose jobs during the Depression made some young people leave school. Many felt they had to go to work to earn some money for their families. In 1936, alarmed about what would happen to these young adults, Eleanor asked the president and Congress to start a National Youth Administration (NYA). The NYA gave money to students who stayed in high school and helped pay college expenses for many others.

Girls attend class on the first day of a Chicago boarding school, opened by the National Youth Administration (NYA), an organization that Eleanor helped form.

Eleanor also convinced the president and Congress to help entire communities. In Scott's Run, a West Virginia town where the coal mines had closed, almost everyone lived in shacks with no running water. The water from the community well tasted like rotten eggs, but people drank it anyway. They had no choice.

Built by the federal government's Arthurdale Subsistence Homestead project in 1934, this house replaced a rundown shack. The yard gave children a place to play.

To help out, the government built new homes with indoor plumbing and large back yards for growing vegetables. Businesses moved to the area, now called Arthurdale, creating jobs for some of the people.

Remembering Others

Fletcher Collins, a resident of Arthurdale, remembered that Eleanor Roosevelt made many friends there. When someone greeted her during a visit, Eleanor replied "Oh, hello, Mrs. Degalier, how are you doing? Your son, he had the measles last time I was here."

Fletcher Collins, speaking on *The American Experience: Eleanor Roosevelt*

Eleanor Fights for Civil Rights

When Eleanor served as first lady, few southern African Americans were allowed to vote, even though they had the right to. Many public places—restaurants, hotels, and even schools—practised segregation, separating blacks and whites. Many northern cities forced blacks to live in run-down homes in segregated neighborhoods. Eleanor's fight against these conditions led to better housing and integrated schools.

During the Depression, Eleanor helped ensure that Works Program Administration (WPA) projects included African Americans. Here, Eleanor visits a WPA nursery school in Des Moines, Iowa, in 1936.

Eleanor's friendship with Mary McLeod Bethune, a black college president, helped Eleanor understand African-American issues. In 1939, the two attended a meeting of the Southern Conference on Human Welfare in Birmingham, Alabama. They were told they could not sit together. Blacks had to sit on one side of the room and whites on the other. Eleanor refused. When a police officer told her she was breaking the law, she had a chair placed in the aisle, between the two sides, and sat there.

Rejecting Prejudice

The Daughters of the American Revolution was a prominent social group of white women whose ancestors had fought in the Revolutionary War. In 1939 they refused to allow the famous singer Marian Anderson (below) to perform at their concert hall just because she was black. Eleanor, a member of the group, arranged for Anderson to perform instead in front of the Lincoln Memorial in Washington, D.C. On Easter Sunday morning, a crowd of 75,000 cheered as Anderson sang "My country 'tis of thee, sweet land of liberty...."

The World at War – Again

On December 7, 1941, Japan attacked the U.S. navy base at Pearl Harbor in Hawaii. The next day the United States entered World War II. Franklin Roosevelt led the country through most of the war. In Europe, the United States, the Soviet Union, and Great Britain battled Germany. Led by the Nazi dictator Adolf Hitler, Germany had conquered much of Europe. In the process, the Nazis had been systematically exterminating the Jewish people. Ultimately, six million were killed by the Nazis, man of them in specially designed death camps.

U.S. Army and Navy nurses stationed in Australia enjoy a visit from first lady Eleanor Roosevelt (in chair) in 1943.

Eleanor Roosevelt was made co-director of the U. S. Office of Civilian Defense. One of her first jobs was to visit American cities on the West Coast, where fears of a Japanese invasion were great. She was one of the few people who protested when Japanese-American civilians were interned in concentration camps. Her view was not very popular at the time.

Eleanor surveys damage in war-torn London. During World War II, Eleanor journeyed around the world, offering support and gathering information.

Acting as her husband's eyes and ears, Eleanor traveled to Europe's battlefields and cities, surveying the damage done by the war. In 1943, she hopped aboard a small, unheated plane and flew thousands of miles to the South Pacific to talk to U.S. soldiers stationed there.

All over the world

The stress of her travels during World War II caused Eleanor to lose 30 pounds. She journeyed so far so often that the famous polar explorer Admiral Richard Byrd joked that he kept a place at the table set just for her at his station in Antarctica.

Battling Until the End

Franklin Roosevelt died on April 12, 1945 soon after suffering a stroke. Harry S. Truman succeeded him as president as the United States finally defeated first Germany and then Japan. After the war, Truman chose Eleanor as a U.S. representative to the new United Nations (U.N.), which was started to help keep peace throughout the world. The U.N. asked Eleanor to help write its Declaration of Human Rights, which would state everyone's right to an education, a fair trial, food, and housing. The U.N. members approved the declaration on December 10, 1948. Recognizing her achievement, the U.N. general assembly clapped in her honor.

Eleanor at work at the U.N., where she again proved herself to be a courageous political leader.

After leaving the U.N. in 1952, Eleanor helped Adlai Stevenson's unsuccessful campaign for the U.S. presidency in 1952. She fought for the 1954 Supreme Court ruling that outlawed segregation in public schools. When John F. Kennedy ran for president in 1960, Eleanor helped him win the election.

Eleanor with President John F. Kennedy, who reappointed her to the U.N. He also appointed her chair of the President's Commission on the Status of Women in 1961.

Eleanor died on November 7, 1962, at the age of 78. Her hard work had produced many positive changes for poor people, women, children, and African Americans.

Prominent black educator Mary McLeod Bethune chats with Eleanor Roosevelt in 1948. Eleanor fought for civil rights all her life.

Embracing Life

"Life was meant to be lived and curiosity must be kept alive. One must never, for whatever reason, turn his back on life."

The Autobiography of Eleanor Roosevelt

Timeline

1884 – October 11 – Anna Eleanor Roosevelt is born in New York City.

1892 – Eleanor's mother, Anna Hall Roosevelt, dies.

1894 – Eleanor's father, Elliott Roosevelt, dies.

1899-1902 – Eleanor attends Allenswood School in England.

1903-04 – Eleanor works with immigrants in the slums of New York City. She joins the Consumers' League to help improve factory conditions.

1905 – March 17 – Eleanor marries Franklin D. Roosevelt.

1906 – Eleanor and Franklin's first child, Anna, is born on May 3.

1907 – Eleanor and Franklin's second child, James, is born on December 23.

1909 – Franklin, Jr., Eleanor and Franklin's third child, is born. He dies of influenza seven months later.

1912 – Eleanor attends her first Democratic Party Convention, which sparks her life-long interest in politics.

1914 – Eleanor and Franklin's fifth child, the second Franklin, Jr., is born on August 17.

1917 – The United States enters World War I.

1920 – Eleanor joins the League of Women Voters.

1921 – After Franklin Roosevelt is stricken with polio, Eleanor encourages him to return to public life.

1925 – Val-Kill Cottage in Hyde Park, New York, is built. It becomes a retreat home for Eleanor and her close women friends.

1926 – Eleanor begins teaching at Todhunter School, a girl's school in New York City.

1933 – Eleanor becomes first lady. She holds the first press conference for women reporters on March 6.

1935 – Eleanor starts publishing her newspaper column, "My Day," which she writes until her death.

1939 – Eleanor helps arrange the Marian Anderson concert on the steps of the Lincoln Memorial in Washington, D.C.

1941 – The United States enters World War II.

1943 – Eleanor travels to the South Pacific to visit U.S. soldiers.

1945 – Franklin Roosevelt dies. President Harry S. Truman appoints Eleanor as a U.S. delegate to the United Nations.

1948 – Eleanor leads the U.N. effort to draft the Universal Declaration of Human Rights.

1952 – Eleanor supports Adlai Stevenson in his unsuccessful attempt to win the U.S. presidency.

1957 – On behalf of the *New York Post*, Eleanor travels to the Soviet Union. She meets with its leader, Nikita Khrushchev.

1960 – Eleanor takes an active role in John F. Kennedy's campaign for the U.S. presidency.

1961 – President Kennedy reappoints Eleanor to the U.N.

1962 – Eleanor dies in New York City on November 7.

Glossary

Civil rights (SIV-il RITES) Legal rights of a citizen.

Curiosity (kyur-ee-AHSS-i-tee)A desire to learn or know.

Drought (DROUT) A long period with little or no rain.

Exterminating (ek-STUR-muh-nate-ing) Completely destroying.

Humanitarian (hyoo-man-uh-TER-ee-uhn) A person who works for social changes that help people.

Immigrants (IM-uh-gruhnts) People who leave one country to live in another.

Integrated (IN-tuh-gra-ted) Open to people of all races.

Interned (IN-turned) Confined, or kept in one place.

Livelihood (LIVE-lee-hud) How someone earns a living.

Nazis (NOT-seez) The Nationalist Socialist party, headed by Adolf Hitler, which came to power in Germany in 1933.

Polio (POH-lee-oh) A disease that attacks the nervous system and often makes it impossible for the sufferer to move certain parts of their bodies (such as legs).

Sanctuary (SANGK-choo-er-ee) A quiet and private place.

Segregation (seg-ruh-GAY-shuhn) Separating people by race or skin color.

Sharecroppers (SHAIR-KROP-ers) Farmers who give a share of their crops to the land owner as rent.

Stroke (STROHK) A sudden loss of brain function caused by the bursting of a blood vessel to the brain.

Further Reading and Information

Books to Read

Adler, David A. *A Picture Book of Eleanor Roosevelt.* New York: Holiday House, 1991.

Cooney, Barbara. *Eleanor.* New York: Viking, 1996.

Davis, Lucile. *Eleanor Roosevelt: A Photo-Illustrated Biography.* Mankato, MN: Bridgestone Books, 1998.

Freedman, Russell. *Eleanor Roosevelt – A Life of Discovery.* New York: Clarion Books, 1993.

Kruss, Kathleen. *Lives of Extraordinary Women.* New York: Harcourt, Inc., 2000.

Morey, Eileen. *Eleanor Roosevelt.* San Diego: Lucent Books, 1998.

Ryan, Pam Munoz. *Amelia and Eleanor Go for a Ride: Based on a True Story.* New York: Scholastic Press, 1999.

Videos

American Experience: Eleanor Roosevelt. PBS Home Video, 2000.

Biography—Eleanor Roosevelt. A & E Entertainment, 1995

The Eleanor Roosevelt Story. Kino Video, 1997.

Index